P9-CCK-071

# POOH'S BIRTHDAY BOOK

OTHER YEARLING BOOKS YOU WILL ENJOY:

*The Pooh Party Book*, VIRGINIA H. ELLISON

*The Pooh Cook Book*, VIRGINIA H. ELLISON

*The Pooh Get-Well Book*, VIRGINIA H. ELLISON

*Winnie-the-Pooh*, A. A. MILNE

*The House at Pooh Corner*, A. A. MILNE

*When We Were Very Young*, A. A. MILNE

*Now We Are Six*, A. A. MILNE

*The Secret Garden*, FRANCES HODGSON BURNETT

*A Little Princess*, FRANCES HODGSON BURNETT

*The Tough Winter*, ROBERT LAWSON

YEARLING BOOKS are designed especially to entertain and enlighten young people. The finest available books for children have been selected under the direction of Charles F. Reasoner, Professor of Elementary Education, New York University.

For a complete listing of all Yearling titles,
write to Education Sales Department, Dell Publishing Co., Inc.,
1 Dag Hammarskjold Plaza, New York, N.Y. 10017

# Pooh's Birthday Book

by A. A. MILNE

Drawings by E. H. Shepard

A YEARLING BOOK

Published by
Dell Publishing Co., Inc.
1 Dag Hammarskjold Plaza
New York, New York 10017

Compilation and illustrations Copyright, © 1963,
by E. P. Dutton & Co., Inc.

All rights reserved. No part of this book may be reproduced in any
form without permission in writing from E. P. Dutton & Co., Inc.,
New York, New York 10003, except by a reviewer who wishes to quote
brief passages in connection with a review written for inclusion in
a magazine, newspaper, or broadcast.

Individual Copyrights:
THE CHRISTOPHER ROBIN BIRTHDAY BOOK
Copyright, 1931, by E. P. Dutton & Co., Inc.
Copyright Renewal, © 1959, by Daphne Milne

WHEN WE WERE VERY YOUNG
Copyright, 1924, by E. P. Dutton & Co., Inc.
Copyright Renewal, 1952, by A. A. Milne

WINNIE-THE-POOH
Copyright, 1926, by E. P. Dutton & Co., Inc.
Copyright Renewal, 1954, by A. A. Milne

NOW WE ARE SIX
Copyright, 1927, by E. P. Dutton & Co., Inc.
Copyright Renewal, © 1955, by A. A. Milne

THE HOUSE AT POOH CORNER
Copyright, 1928, by E. P. Dutton & Co., Inc.
Copyright Renewal, © 1956, by A. A. Milne

Yearling ® TM 913705, Dell Publishing Co., Inc.
ISBN: 0-440-46934-1
Reprinted by arrangement with E. P. Dutton & Co., Inc.
Printed in the United States of America

Fifth Dell Printing—March 1979

CW

# INTRODUCTION

As Eeyore says, "What are birthdays? Here to-day and gone tomorrow." So let us make a note of them while we can. Of course it would be pleasanter if other people made a note of ours in their books, rather than called attention to their own in ours, but, even so, if we are careful to write to our Uncle Henry for the 20th of October, wishing him many happy returns, and mentioning casually the coincidence that our birthday is exactly seventeen days later than his, we may find ourselves in the pleasing position of having to write to him again before November is out.

If the English Language had been properly organized by a Business Man or Member of Parliament, instead of living from hand to mouth on almost anybody who happened to be about with a pencil, then there would be a word which meant both "he" *and* "she," and I could write, "If John or Mary comes, heesh will want to play tennis," which would save a lot of trouble. Also I could have made a much better thing of this Birthday Book. As it is, most of the quotations refer definitely to one sex, and more often to "he" than to "she." But you must not let this worry you. If Aunt Emily's birthday is on December 7th—well, no, let us hope it isn't; but if it were on April 2nd —no, that's wrong. Well, what I mean is that the motto for June 20th, "*He*'ll know what to do," can be read, if necessary, as "*She*'ll know what to do," and so on and so forth, and vice versa and otherwise. I hope that's clear.

One other suggestion. If you buy this book at all, or if anybody gives it to you, it can only be because you are friendly with the four books from which I have taken the mottoes. If that is so, then you can amuse yourself (when you've got *absolutely* nothing to do) by trying to guess from which chapter or verse of a book each quotation comes. With some you will have no difficulty; others will baffle you for a long time, even if you start looking through the books carefully for them. But, of course, if the sun is shining and you can do anything else, I should strongly advise you to do it.

A. A. M.

## How to Use This Book

FIRST, ask all the members of your family and all your aunts, uncles, cousins, and grandparents to read the quotation for the day they were born—and to sign their name on that day. Next ask all your friends to do the same. Now you'll have a record of birthdays that you can use year after year. You'll never forget to wish someone "Many happy returns of the day!" And no friend or relation will ever feel as Eeyore did—as you may remember, he was in a Very Sad Condition because it was his birthday, and nobody had taken any notice of it.

If you follow these instructions you'll discover right away why *Pooh's Birthday Book* is a Useful Book to Keep Birth Dates In.

# JANUARY

If you were a bird, and lived on high,
You'd lean on the wind when the wind came by,
You'd say to the wind when it took you away:
"*That's* where I wanted to go today!"

*When We Were Very Young*

If I were King of anything,
I'd tell the soldiers, "I'm the King!"

*When We Were Very Young*

[2]

On Tuesday when it hails and snows,
The feeling on me grows and grows
That hardly anybody knows
If those are these or these are those.

*Winnie-the-Pooh*

[3]

The Knight Whose Armour Didn't Squeak!

*Now We Are Six*

She would do a Good Thing to Do without thinking about it.

*Winnie-the-Pooh*

[5]

"What would I do?" I said to Pooh,
"If it wasn't for you," and Pooh said: "True."

*Now We Are Six*

[6]

"Pooh!" cried Piglet, and now it was *his* turn to be the admiring one. "You've saved us!"

*The House at Pooh Corner*

. . . whose life was made up of Important Things.

*The House at Pooh Corner*

[8]

Have you been a *good* girl?

*Now We Are Six*

[9]

Astute and Helpful Bear.

*The House at Pooh Corner*

"What sort of stories does he like?"
"About himself. Because he's *that* sort of Bear."

*Winnie-the-Pooh*

[11]

very calm, very dignified.

*The House at Pooh Corner*

[12]

If I were Emperors,
   If I were Kings,
It couldn't be fuller
   Of wonderful things.

*Now We Are Six*

Nobody,
My darling,
Could call me
A fussy man.

*When We Were Very Young*

[14]

They heard a deep gruff voice saying in a singing voice that the more it snowed the more it went on snowing and a small high voice tiddely-pomming in between.

*The House at Pooh Corner*

[15]

What has she got in that little brown head?
Wonderful thoughts which can never be said.

*Now We Are Six*

The snow, tired of rushing around in circles trying
to catch itself up, now fluttered gently down.

*The House at Pooh Corner*

[17]

You'll be quite safe with *him.*

*Winnie-the-Pooh*

[18]

Who comes tripping round the corner
 of the street?

*When We Were Very Young*

I don't hold with all this washing. . . . This modern
Behind-the-ears nonsense.

*Winnie-the-Pooh*

[20]

When Anne and I go out a walk,
We hold each other's hand and talk
Of all the things we mean to do
When Anne and I are forty-two.

*Now We Are Six*

[21]

It's my birthday. The happiest day of the year.

*Winnie-the-Pooh*

Amusing in a quiet way. . . .

*The House at Pooh Corner*

[23]

"They don't hurt themselves," said Pooh. "They're such very good droppers."

*The House at Pooh Corner*

[24]

When I go up the Amazon,
I stop at night and fire a gun
   To call my faithful band.

*When We Were Very Young*

Delighted to meet you here!

*When We Were Very Young*

[26]

Halfway down the stairs
Is a stair
Where I sit.

*When We Were Very Young*

[27]

The only reason for making honey is so as *I* can
eat it.

*Winnie-the-Pooh*

He gets what exercise he can
By falling off the ottoman.

*When We Were Very Young*

[29]

Look at the birthday cake. Candles and pink sugar.

*Winnie-the-Pooh*

[30]

One of those Clever Readers who can read things.

*Winnie-the-Pooh*

And the look in his eye
Seemed to say to the sky,
*"Now, how to amuse them today?"*

*Now We Are Six*

# FEBRUARY

And nobody knows
      (Tiddely pom),
How cold my toes
      (Tiddely pom),
How cold my toes
      (Tiddely pom),
   Are growing.

*The House at Pooh Corner*

I only came to oblige. But here I am.

*Winnie-the-Pooh*

[2]

I can think whatever I like to think,
I can play whatever I like to play,
I can laugh whatever I like to laugh.

*Now We Are Six*

[3]

"You only blinched inside," said Pooh, "and that's the bravest way for a Very Small Animal not to blinch that there is."

*The House at Pooh Corner*

"*I'm* not afraid," I said to Pooh,
  And I held his paw and I shouted "Shoo!
Silly old dragons!"—and off they flew.

*Now We Are Six*

[5]

I have a house where I go
  When there's too many people,
I have a house where I go
  Where no one can be.

*Now We Are Six*

[6]

He sat down and thought, in the most thoughtful
way he could think.

*Winnie-the-Pooh*

I don't much care if it snows or thaws,
'Cos I've got a lot of honey on my nice clean paws!

*Winnie-the-Pooh*

[8]

All sorts of funny thoughts
Run round my head.

*When We Were Very Young*

[9]

This stranger made a nicer sound
Than other Knights who lived around.

*Now We Are Six*

*Promise* you won't forget about me, ever. Not even when I'm a hundred.

*The House at Pooh Corner*

[11]

You find sometimes that a Thing which seemed very Thingish inside you is quite different when it gets out into the open and has other people looking at it.

*The House at Pooh Corner*

[12]

E.C. and T.F. (Eeyore's Comforter and Tail-finder).

*Winnie-the-Pooh*

He doesn't use long, difficult words, like Owl.

*The House at Pooh Corner*

[14]

I'll love you for ever and ever,
    Little Bo-Peep.
I'll love you for ever and ever,
    Bo-Peep.

*When We Were Very Young*

[15]

*He did a hundred happy things—*
*And then went to bed.*

*Now We Are Six*

"Are you," he said, "by any chance
His Majesty the King of France?"

*When We Were Very Young*

[17]

I think that he sounds so exciting.

*When We Were Very Young*

[18]

I'm not frightened of Fierce Animals in the ordinary way.

*Winnie-the-Pooh*

I am going to give a party.

*Winnie-the-Pooh*

[20]

It's just the day for doing things.

**The House at Pooh Corner**

[21]

He thought it would be lovely to be able to fly.

**The House at Pooh Corner**

You're the Best Bear in All the World.

*Winnie-the-Pooh*

[23]

I don't much mind if it rains or
    snows,
'Cos I've got a lot of honey on my
    nice new nose.

*Winnie-the-Pooh*

[24]

You're the only one who seems to understand
about tails.

*Winnie-the-Pooh*

There are lots and lots of people who are always
   asking things,
Like Dates and Pounds-and-ounces and the names
   of funny Kings. . . .

*Now We Are Six*

[26]

The little fellow with the excited ears.

*Winnie-the-Pooh*

[27]

*Will be, as sure as eggs are eggs,*
   *A Chancellor some day.*

*Now We Are Six*

There is in my old picture-book
A page at which I like to look,
Where knights and squires come riding down
The cobbles of some steep old town.

*When We Were Very Young*

[29]

A very happy birthday, with love from Pooh.

*Winnie-the-Pooh*

# MARCH

*For lo! the wind was blusterous.*

*The House at Pooh Corner*

Where am I going? The high rooks call:
"It's awful fun to be born at all."

*When We Were Very Young*

[2]

Quiet and Refined.

*The House at Pooh Corner*

[3]

He talks about sensible things.

*The House at Pooh Corner*

She wore her yellow sun-bonnet,
  She wore her greenest gown;
She turned to the south wind
  And curtsied up and down.

*When We Were Very Young*

[5]

*There's wind on the river and wind on the hill.*
*Now We Are Six*

[6]

There's really nobody but Me, when you come to
look at it.

*The House at Pooh Corner*

A Bear with a Pleasing Manner . . .

*The House at Pooh Corner*

[8]

Of all the Knights in Appledore
The wisest was Sir Thomas Tom.

*Now We Are Six*

[9]

I never did, I never did, I never *did* like
"Now take care, dear!"

*When We Were Very Young*

All the streams of the Forest were tinkling happily.
*Winnie-the-Pooh*

[11]

Christopher Robin depends on Me.
*The House at Pooh Corner*

[12]

. . . I could tell them
   Where the wind goes . . .
But where the wind comes from
   *Nobody* knows.

*Now We Are Six*

I saw a Heffalump to-day.

*Winnie-the-Pooh*

[14]

If you ask for a bat
Or something like that,
He has got it, whatever the size is.

*When We Were Very Young*

[15]

Oh, the butterflies are flying,
Now the winter days are dying,
And the primroses are trying
    To be seen.

*The House at Pooh Corner*

"It isn't much fun for One, but Two
   Can stick together," says Pooh, says he.
"That's how it is," says Pooh.

*Now We Are Six*

[17]

No one can tell me,
   Nobody knows,
Where the wind comes from,
   Where the wind goes.

*Now We Are Six*

[18]

Well, he was humming this hum to himself, and
walking along gaily, wondering what everybody
else was doing, and what it felt like, being somebody else . . .

*Winnie-the-Pooh*

"It's a remarkable thing," he said. "It *is* my house . . . the wind must have blown it here . . . Here it is as good as ever. In fact, better in places."

*The House at Pooh Corner*

He got close up to Pooh and felt much braver.

*The House at Pooh Corner*

Then all the wood began to sing
Its morning anthem to the spring.

*When We Were Very Young*

He can always Think of a Clever Plan.

*Winnie-the-Pooh*

[23]

Whenever I'm a shining Knight,
I buckle on my armour tight.

*Now We Are Six*

[24]

I wonder what's going to happen exciting *to-day*.

*Winnie-the-Pooh*

. . . dreaming of the life they had seen and the big things they had done.

*Winnie-the-Pooh*

[26]

". . . when you've been walking in the wind for miles, and you suddenly go into somebody's house, and he says, 'Hallo, Pooh, you're just in time for a little smackerel of something,' and you are, then it's what I call a Friendly Day."

*The House at Pooh Corner*

[27]

"Me having a real Birthday?"

*Winnie-the-Pooh*

We are all going on an Expedition.
*Winnie-the-Pooh*

[29]

"It is hard to be brave," said Piglet, sniffing
slightly, "when you're only a Very Small Animal."
*Winnie-the-Pooh*

[30]

So now let's give him three hearty cheers
And hope he'll be with us for years and years.
*Winnie-the-Pooh*

Where am I going? I don't quite know:
What does it matter where people go?

*When We Were Very Young*

## APRIL

All the things they have seen,
All the things they have heard:
An April sky swept clean and the
song of a bird . . .

*Now We Are Six*

And rabbits come up and say, "Beautiful morning."

*Now We Are Six*

[2]

Then would you read a Sustaining Book, such as would help and comfort a Wedged Bear in Tightness?

*Winnie-the-Pooh*

[3]

Not only did he understand
   The way to polish swords, but knew
What remedy a Knight should seek
Whose armour had begun to squeak.

*Now We Are Six*

"I wasn't afraid," said Pooh, said he,
"I'm *never* afraid with you."

*Now We Are Six*

[5]

If there is any thinking to be done in this Forest
—and when I say thinking, I mean *thinking*—you
and I must do it.

*The House at Pooh Corner*

[6]

There's nobody else in the world, and the world
was made for me.

*When We Were Very Young*

F.O.P. (Friend of Piglet's).

*Winnie-the-Pooh*

[8]

For the spring is really springing;
You can see a skylark singing,
And the blue-bells, which are ringing,
    Can be heard.

*The House at Pooh Corner*

[9]

Most faithful of all my Knights.

*The House at Pooh Corner*

They've great big parties inside the grounds.
*When We Were Very Young*

[11]

But they were all quite happy when Pooh and Piglet came along, and they stopped working in order
to have a little rest and listen to Pooh's new song.
*The House at Pooh Corner*

[12]

If you were a cloud, and sailed up there,
  You'd sail on water as blue as air,
  And you'd see me here in the fields and say:
"Doesn't the sky look green today?"
*When We Were Very Young*

You and I have brains. The others have fluff.

*The House at Pooh Corner*

[14]

This warm and sunny Spot
  Belongs to Pooh.
And here he wonders what
  He's going to do.

*The House at Pooh Corner*

[15]

I say to them, "Bears,
Just look how I'm walking in all of the squares!"

*When We Were Very Young*

It was a fine spring morning in the forest.

*Winnie-the-Pooh*

[17]

*"Getting Tigger down,"* said Eeyore, "and *Not hurting anybody.* Keep those two ideas in your head, Piglet, and you'll be all right."

*The House at Pooh Corner*

[18]

. . . he laughed . . . and he laughed . . . and he laughed.

*Winnie-the-Pooh*

I am Sir Brian, as bold as a lion—

*When We Were Very Young*

[20]

Sing Ho! for the life of a Bear.

*Winnie-the-Pooh*

[21]

And the turtle-doves are cooing,
And the woods are up and doing,
For the violets are blue-ing
    In the green.

*The House at Pooh Corner*

Nobody can be uncheered with a balloon.
*Winnie-the-Pooh*

[23]

Where am I going? I don't quite know.
Down to the stream where the king-cups grow—
Up on the hill where the pine-trees blow—
Anywhere, anywhere. *I* don't know.
*When We Were Very Young*

[24]

"Does Christopher Robin know about you?"
"Of course he does."
*The House at Pooh Corner*

One day, when Pooh was walking towards this bridge, he was trying to make up a piece of poetry about fir-cones, because there they were, lying about on each side of him, and he felt singy.

*The House at Pooh Corner*

[26]

If I were King of Norroway
I'd ask an elephant to stay.

*When We Were Very Young*

[27]

What you have just said will be a Great Help to us.

*The House at Pooh Corner*

"Where are you going this fine day?"
(I said to the Puppy as he went by).

*When We Were Very Young*

[29]

A soldier's life is terrible hard.

*When We Were Very Young*

[30]

He was feeling particularly cheerful this morning.

*The House at Pooh Corner*

# MAY

In careless patches through the wood
The clumps of yellow primrose stood.

*When We Were Very Young*

The sun had come back over the Forest, bringing
with it the scent of May.

*Winnie-the-Pooh*

[2]

Cottleston, Cottleston, Cottleston Pie,
A fly can't bird, but a bird can fly.
Ask me a riddle and I reply:
"*Cottleston, Cottleston, Cottleston Pie.*"

*Winnie-the-Pooh*

[3]

. . . feeling all sunny and careless, and just as if
twice nineteen didn't matter a bit.

*The House at Pooh Corner*

Do you think the King knows all about *me?*
                              *When We Were Very Young*

[5]

He ran after butterflies,
  Blue ones and red.

*Now We Are Six*

[6]

My spelling is Wobbly. It's good spelling, but it
Wobbles and the letters get in the wrong places.
                              *Winnie-the-Pooh*

If John were Me, and I were John,
I shouldn't have these trousers on.

*Now We Are Six*

[8]

He would know the Right Thing to Do when
Surrounded by Water.

*Winnie-the-Pooh*

[9]

I could spend a happy morning
   Seeing Roo,
I could spend a happy morning
   Being Pooh.

*The House at Pooh Corner*

And Indians in twos and threes,
Come silently between the trees,
    And wait for me to land.

*When We Were Very Young*

[11]

    However much you liked him, you couldn't deny it, he *did* bounce.

*The House at Pooh Corner*

[12]

Pooh went back to his own house, and feeling very proud of what he had done, had a little something to revive himself.

*Winnie-the-Pooh*

Why, the more that you ask for, the merrier—
    Like a hoop and a top,
    And a watch that won't stop,
And some sweets, and an Aberdeen terrier.
*When We Were Very Young*

[14]

What a Brave and Clever Bear
*Winnie-the-Pooh*

[15]

Breathing the early morning air
And leaving it still sweeter there.
*When We Were Very Young*

Oh, there's such a lot of things to do
  and such a lot to be.

*Now We Are Six*

[17]

HIPY PAPY BTHUTHDTH THUTHDA
BTHUTHDY.

*Winnie-the-Pooh*

[18]

We can look for the North Pole, or we can play
"Here we go gathering Nuts and May."

*Winnie-the-Pooh*

On Wednesday, when the sky is blue,
And I have nothing else to do,
I sometimes wonder if it's true
That who is what and what is who.

*Winnie-the-Pooh*

[20]

*There's sun on the river and sun on the hill.*

*Now We Are Six*

[21]

. . . isn't greedy, but he does like things to eat.

*Now We Are Six*

"If anybody wants to clap, . . . now is the time to do it."

*The House at Pooh Corner*

[23]

My lady is marrying her own true knight,
White her gown, and her veil is white.

*When We Were Very Young*

[24]

Christopher Robin goes
Hoppity, hoppity,
Hoppity, hoppity hop.

*When We Were Very Young*

---

*I do like a little bit of butter to my bread.*
*When We Were Very Young*

[26]

---

A Bear of Enormous Brain,
 (*Just say it again*),
Of Enormous Brain.

*Winnie-the-Pooh*

[27]

---

I look out for things,
Like Rushings-Out, and Rescuings.

*Now We Are Six*

I wouldn't be King for a hundred pounds.

*When We Were Very Young*

[29]

And the cuckoo isn't cooing,
But he's cucking and he's ooing,
And a Pooh is simply poohing
    Like a bird.

*The House at Pooh Corner*

[30]

Kind and Thoughtful.

*Winnie-the-Pooh*

Where am I going? The ring-doves coo:
"We do have beautiful things to do."

*When We Were Very Young*

# JUNE

When the sun
Shines through the leaves of the apple-tree,
When the sun
Makes shadows of the leaves of the apple-tree,
Then I pass
On the grass
From one leaf to another.

*When We Were Very Young*

Oh, the honey-bees are gumming
On their little wings, and humming
That the summer, which is coming,
    Will be fun.

*The House at Pooh Corner*

[2]

I *am* so fond of him.

*When We Were Very Young*

[3]

He thought of himself floating on his back down
a river, or striking out from one island to another,
and he felt that that was really the life for a Tigger.

*The House at Pooh Corner*

I think to myself,
I play to myself,
And nobody knows what I say to myself.

*Now We Are Six*

[5]

Where is Anne?
   Head above the buttercups,
Walking by the stream,
   Down among the buttercups.

*Now We Are Six*

[6]

"I'm just saying 'A Happy Birthday,'" said Owl
carelessly.

*Winnie-the-Pooh*

*Whatever Fortune brings,*
*Don't be afraid of doing things.*

*Now We Are Six*

[8]

Wherever I am, there's always Pooh,
There's always Pooh and Me.

*Now We Are Six*

[9]

. . . had never been really
fond of baths . . .

*Winnie-the-Pooh*

"And if anyone knows anything about anything,"
said Bear to himself, "it's Owl who knows something about something."

*Winnie-the-Pooh*

[11]

*Shall I go off to South America?*
  *Shall I put out in my ship to sea?*
*Or get in my cage and be lions and tigers?*
  *Or—shall I be only Me?*

*When We Were Very Young*

[12]

There are twelve pots of honey in my cupboard,
and they've been calling to me for hours.

*The House at Pooh Corner*

No other Knight in all the land
  Could do the things which he could do.

*Now We Are Six*

[14]

What *will* he be doing next?

*Winnie-the-Pooh*

[15]

And the cows are almost cooing,
And the turtle-doves are mooing,
Which is why a Pooh is poohing
      In the sun.

*The House at Pooh Corner*

It's so much more friendly with two.

*Winnie-the-Pooh*

[17]

On such a day as this Christopher Robin whistled
in a special way he had.

*Winnie-the-Pooh*

[18]

Apple-cheeked, dimpled. . . .

*Now We Are Six*

He thought: "It really isn't fair
To grudge me exercise and air."

*When We Were Very Young*

[20]

*He'll* know what to do.

*The House at Pooh Corner*

[21]

With a laugh she is slipping
Through the lilies on the water.

*When We Were Very Young*

I'm all ready to run some races.
    Who's coming out with me?

*When We Were Very Young*

[23]

I go to a party, I go out to tea,
I go to an aunt for a week at the sea,
I come back from school or from playing a game;
Wherever I come from, it's always the same:
    "Well?
    Have you been a *good* girl, Jane?"

*Now We Are Six*

[24]

"Enjoy yourself."
"I am," said Pooh.
"Some can," said Eeyore.

*Winnie-the-Pooh*

He had thought of it without being told by anybody.

*Winnie-the-Pooh*

[26]

What I like *doing* best is Nothing.

*The House at Pooh Corner*

[27]

And I sometimes call him Terrible James,
'Cos he says he likes me calling him names.

*When We Were Very Young*

Tip-toe, tip-toe!
Here I go!

*When We Were Very Young*

[29]

Perhaps it's some relation of Pooh's.

*Winnie-the-Pooh*

[30]

Pooh went into a corner of the room and said proudly to himself, "Impossible without Me! *That* sort of Bear."

*Winnie-the-Pooh*

# JULY

For a long time they looked at the river beneath them, saying nothing, and the river said nothing too, for it felt very quiet and peaceful on this summer afternoon.

*The House at Pooh Corner*

We had sand in the eyes and the ears and the nose,
And sand in the hair, and sand-between-the-toes.

*When We Were Very Young*

[2]

All of a sudden Piglet felt that it was a much nicer day than he had thought it was.

*The House at Pooh Corner*

[3]

Where is Anne?
Close to her man.
Brown head, gold head,
    In and out the buttercups.

*Now We Are Six*

You can hear the sea if you stand quite still!

*Now We Are Six*

[5]

Only fierce during the winter months.

*Winnie-the-Pooh*

[6]

James James
Said to his Mother,
"Mother," he said, said he:
"You must never go down to the end of the town,
if you don't go down with me."

*When We Were Very Young*

He could see the honey, he could smell the honey,
but he couldn't quite reach the honey.

*Winnie-the-Pooh*

[8]

On Monday, when the sun is hot
I wonder to myself a lot:
"Now, is it true, or is it not,
That what is which and which is what?"

*Winnie-the-Pooh*

[9]

Who had so many things which he wanted to do . . .

*Now We Are Six*

Many a bear going out on a warm day like this would never have thought of bringing a little something with him.

*Winnie-the-Pooh*

[11]

Then I'd leave my ship and I'd land,
And climb the steep white sand . . .

*When We Were Very Young*

[12]

Look at me swimming!

*Winnie-the-Pooh*

Binker's brave as lions when we're running in the
   park;
Binker's brave as tigers when we're lying in the
   dark. . . .

*Now We Are Six*

[14]

I generally have a small something about now—
about this time in the morning.

*Winnie-the-Pooh*

[15]

Pooh had once invented a song which went:
   *Tra-la-la, tra-la-la,*
   *Tra-la-la, tra-la-la,*
   *Rum-tum-tum-tiddle-um.*

*The House at Pooh Corner*

"I *love* jumping," said Roo. "Let's see who can jump farthest, you or me."

*The House at Pooh Corner*

[17]

Eeyore, who is a friend of mine, has lost his tail.

*Winnie-the-Pooh*

[18]

"And I know it *seems* easy," said Piglet to himself, "but it isn't *every one* who could do it."

*The House at Pooh Corner*

Cottleston, Cottleston, Cottleston Pie,
A fish can't whistle and neither can I.
Ask me a riddle and I reply:
*"Cottleston, Cottleston, Cottleston Pie."*

*Winnie-the-Pooh*

[20]

And the sun comes slanting between the trees,
And rabbits come up, and they give him good-
morning.

*Now We Are Six*

[21]

He hurried out again, saying to himself, "Eeyore,
Violets," and then "Violets, Eeyore," in case he
forgot, because it was that sort of day.

*The House at Pooh Corner*

About as big as Piglet . . . My favourite size.

*Winnie-the-Pooh*

[23]

He stopped and listened, and everything stopped
and listened with him, and the Forest was very
lone and still and peaceful in the sunshine, until
suddenly a hundred miles above him a lark began
to sing.

*The House at Pooh Corner*

[24]

I have just remembered something that I forgot
to do yesterday, and shan't be able to do to-
morrow.

*Winnie-the-Pooh*

But whatever his weight in pounds, shillings, and
  ounces,
He always seems bigger because of his bounces.

*The House at Pooh Corner*

[26]

Many happy returns of the day.

*Winnie-the-Pooh*

[27]

When I am in my ship, I see
  The other ships go sailing by.
A sailor leans and calls to me
  As his ship goes sailing by.

*When We Were Very Young*

All the little streams higher up in the Forest went this way and that, quickly, eagerly, having so much to find out before it was too late.

*The House at Pooh Corner*

[29]

He thought that if he stood on the bottom rail of the bridge, and leant over, and watched the river slipping slowly away beneath him, then he would suddenly know everything that there was to be known.

*The House at Pooh Corner*

[30]

I think I am a Muffin Man. I haven't got a bell, I haven't got the muffin things that muffin people sell.

*Now We Are Six*

. . . being as helpful as possible.

*Winnie-the-Pooh*

## AUGUST

The sun was so delightfully warm, and the stone, which had been sitting in it for a long time, was so warm, too, that Pooh had almost decided to go on being Pooh in the middle of the stream for the rest of the morning.

*The House at Pooh Corner*

Piglet had got up early that morning to pick him-self a bunch of violets; and . . . it suddenly came over him that nobody had ever picked Eeyore a bunch of violets.

*The House at Pooh Corner*

[2]

You're a real friend.

*Winnie-the-Pooh*

[3]

How brave and clever you are.

*The House at Pooh Corner*

"But is it really your birthday?" he asked.
"It is."
"Oh! Well, Many happy returns of the day."

*Winnie-the-Pooh*

[5]

A Very Bouncy Animal, with a way of saying
How-do-you-do, which always left your ears full of
sand. . . .

*The House at Pooh Corner*

[6]

Sometimes he thought sadly to himself, "Why?"
and sometimes he thought, "Wherefore?" and
sometimes he thought, "Inasmuch as which?"

*Winnie-the-Pooh*

He played with his skipping rope,
   He played with his ball.

*Now We Are Six*

[8]

Piglet wasn't afraid if he had Christopher Robin
with him, so off they went.

*Winnie-the-Pooh*

[9]

Lost in a dream,
   Lost among the buttercups.

*Now We Are Six*

*. . . where are you going, Christopher Robin?*
"Just up to the top of the hill,
  Upping and upping until
  I am right on the top of the hill,"
                          Said Christopher Robin.
                                  *Now We Are Six*

[11]

If only I were King of France
I wouldn't brush my hair for aunts.
                          *When We Were Very Young*

[12]

He went on with his walk through the forest, humming proudly to himself. But Christopher Robin
looked after him lovingly, and said to himself,
"Silly old Bear!"

                                  *Winnie-the-Pooh*

*Round* about
And *round* about
And *round* about I go—

*Now We Are Six*

[14]

Eeyore led the way to the most thistly-looking patch of thistles that ever was, and waved a hoof at it.

"A little patch I was keeping for my birthday," he said. "Help yourself, Tigger."

*The House at Pooh Corner*

[15]

I wish I could jump like that.

*Winnie-the-Pooh*

I wonder if you've got such a thing as a balloon
about you?

*Winnie-the-Pooh*

[17]

As soon as he woke up he felt important, as if
everything depended upon him.

*The House at Pooh Corner*

[18]

Pooh always liked a little something at eleven
o'clock in the morning.

*Winnie-the-Pooh*

He never, never cries . . .
Except (like other people) when the soap gets in
  his eyes.

*Now We Are Six*

[20]

He put his head between his paws and thought
very carefully.

*Winnie-the-Pooh*

[21]

It was a drowsy summer afternoon, and the Forest
was full of gentle sounds, which all seemed to be
saying to Pooh, "Don't listen to Rabbit, listen to
me."

*The House at Pooh Corner*

And then he had a Clever Idea.

*Winnie-the-Pooh*

[23]

. . . the only one in the forest who could spell.

*Winnie-the-Pooh*

[24]

Whenever I walk in a London street,
I'm ever so careful to watch my feet;

*When We Were Very Young*

. . . of an Affectionate Disposition.

*Winnie-the-Pooh*

[26]

"I can swim," said Roo. "I fell into the river, and I swimmed. Can Tiggers swim?"

"Of course they can. Tiggers can do everything."

**The House at Pooh Corner**

[27]

A sort of funny feeling began to creep all over him. It began at the tip of his nose and trickled all through him and out at the soles of his feet.

*Winnie-the-Pooh*

I can shut one eye,
I can count to ten.

*Now We Are Six*

[29]

. . . careful not to wet his feet.

*Now We Are Six*

[30]

Owl, wise though he was in many ways, able to
read and write and spell his own name WOL, yet
somehow went all to pieces over delicate words
like MEASLES and BUTTERED TOAST.

*Winnie-the-Pooh*

It was just the day for Organizing Something.

*The House at Pooh Corner*

## SEPTEMBER

Gold between the poplars
  And old moon shows;
Silver up the star-way
  The full moon rose.

*Now We Are Six*

I am the King of the earth, and the King
  Of the sky.

*Now We Are Six*

[2]

Will there be those little cake things with pink
sugar icing?

*Winnie-the-Pooh*

[3]

So much for *washing* . . .

*Winnie-the-Pooh*

"Where are you going today?" says Pooh:
"Well, that's very odd 'cos I was too.
Let's go together," says Pooh, says he.
"Let's go together," says Pooh.

*Now We Are Six*

[5]

He does silly things and they turn out right.

*Winnie-the-Pooh*

[6]

Playing in the nursery, sitting on the stair,
Whatever I am busy at, Binker will be there.

*Now We Are Six*

Christopher Robin is giving a party.

*Winnie-the-Pooh*

[8]

It was more fun to lie down . . . and watch the river slipping slowly away beneath him.

*The House at Pooh Corner*

[9]

It was rather exciting.

*Winnie-the-Pooh*

But *I* gave buns to the elephant when *I* went
   down to the Zoo!

*When We Were Very Young*

[11]

Although Eating Honey *was* a very good thing to
do, there was a moment just before you began to
eat it which was better than when you were, but
he didn't know what it was called.

*The House at Pooh Corner*

[12]

  I think *Violets* are rather nice," said Piglet. And
he laid his bunch in front of Eeyore and scampered
off.

*The House at Pooh Corner*

And, one by one, intent upon
Their purposes, they followed on
In ordered silence . . . and were gone.

*When We Were Very Young*

[14]

"Isn't it fun? Pooh, isn't it fun, Tigger and I are
living in a tree, like Owl, and we're going to stay
here for ever and ever."

*The House at Pooh Corner*

[15]

He asks about this, and explains about that.

*When We Were Very Young*

He's just the one person I'm longing to meet.
                    *When We Were Very Young*

[17]

Nicknamed "The Handsome!"
                    *When We Were Very Young*

[18]

You can't help respecting anybody who can spell
TUESDAY, even if he doesn't spell it right.
                    *The House at Pooh Corner*

Many happy returns of Eeyore's birthday.
*Winnie-the-Pooh*

[20]

He had made up a little hum that very morning.
*Winnie-the-Pooh*

[21]

R.C. (Rabbit's Companion)
*Winnie-the-Pooh*

They went to a Fair, and they all won prizes—
Three plum-puddings and three mince-pieses.

*When We Were Very Young*

[23]

And he gave a deep sigh, and tried very hard to
listen to what Owl was saying.

*Winnie-the-Pooh*

[24]

Ready for Anything.

*Winnie-the-Pooh*

What do we do next?

*Winnie-the-Pooh*

[26]

"It just shows what can be done by taking a little trouble," said Eeyore.

*The House at Pooh Corner*

[27]

. . . felt rather motherly that morning, and Wanting to Count things.

*The House at Pooh Corner*

There is an Invitation for you.

*Winnie-the-Pooh*

[29]

I must move about more. I must come and go.

*The House at Pooh Corner*

[30]

A great big fellow.

*When We Were Very Young*

# OCTOBER

And the moon swings clear of the tall black
    trees,
And owls fly over and wish him good-night,
Quietly over to wish him good-night.

*Now We Are Six*

"I'll think a lot to-morrow . . .

*Now We Are Six*

[2]

And it's to be a special sort of party.

*Winnie-the-Pooh*

[3]

At times like these the bravest Knight
May find his armour much too tight.

*Now We Are Six*

A Captainish sort of day.

*The House at Pooh Corner*

[5]

"Let's look for dragons," I said to Pooh.
"Yes, let's," said Pooh to Me.

*Now We Are Six*

[6]

Pooh said "Oh!" and "I didn't know," and thought
how wonderful it would be to have a Real Brain
which could tell you things.

*The House at Pooh Corner*

I'm BRAVE.

*Now We Are Six*

[8]

"Your birthday?" said Pooh in great surprise. "Of course it is. Can't you see?"

*Winnie-the-Pooh*

[9]

He thought that being with Christopher Robin was a very good thing to do, and having Piglet near was a very friendly thing to have.

*The House at Pooh Corner*

Took great
Care of his Mother . . .

*When We Were Very Young*

[11]

For of all the things which he had said Tiggers
could do, the only one he felt certain about suddenly was climbing trees.

*The House at Pooh Corner*

[12]

Very well-intentioned

*When We Were Very Young*

It's always useful to know where a friend-and-relation *is*, whether you want him or whether you don't.

*The House at Pooh Corner*

[14]

I'm not at the bottom,
I'm not at the top.

*When We Were Very Young*

[15]

Pooh looked proud at being called a stout and helpful bear, and said modestly that he just happened to think of it.

*The House at Pooh Corner*

"Oh, Bear!" said Christopher Robin. "How I do love you!"

*Winnie-the-Pooh*

[17]

I have a house where I go,
Where nobody ever says "No";
Where no one says anything—so
   There is no one but me.

*Now We Are Six*

[18]

Coming through pale fawn fluff at about half-past eleven on a very sunny morning, it seemed to Pooh to be one of the best songs he had ever sung. So he went on singing it.

*The House at Pooh Corner*

It rained so hard that he stayed indoors most of the time, and thought about things.

*Winnie-the-Pooh*

[20]

. . . feeling quite happy again now.

*Winnie-the-Pooh*

[21]

If only I were King of Greece
I'd push things off the mantel-piece.

*When We Were Very Young*

It knew now where it was going, and it said to itself, "There is no hurry. We shall get there some day."

*The House at Pooh Corner*

[23]

He jumped up and down to keep warm, and a hum came suddenly into his head, which seemed to him a Good Hum, such as is Hummed Hopefully to Others.

*The House at Pooh Corner*

[24]

"This is Serious," said Pooh. "I must have an Escape."

*Winnie-the-Pooh*

"Well done, Piglet," said Christopher Robin.

And at these encouraging words Piglet felt quite happy again, and decided not to be a Sailor after all.

*The House at Pooh Corner*

[26]

It all comes of *liking* honey so much.

*Winnie-the-Pooh*

[27]

Sitting there they could see the whole world spread out until it reached the sky, and whatever there was all the world over was with them.

*The House at Pooh Corner*

Here I am.

*Winnie-the-Pooh*

[29]

Everybody was doing something to help.

*Winnie-the-Pooh*

[30]

Kanga said very kindly, "Well, look in my cupboard, Tigger dear, and see what you'd like." Because she knew at once that, however big Tigger
seemed to be, he wanted as much kindness as Roo.

*The House at Pooh Corner*

I never did, I never did, I never *did* want
  "Hold-my-hand."

*When We Were Very Young*

## NOVEMBER

In the half-light the Pine-Trees looked cold
and lonely.

*Winnie-the-Pooh*

On Thursday, when it starts to freeze
And hoar-frost twinkles on the trees,
How very readily one sees
That these are whose—but whose are these?

*Winnie-the-Pooh*

[2]

He waved a paw at them over his shoulder, and
was gone; leaving such an air of excitement and
I-don't-know-what behind him.

*The House at Pooh Corner*

[3]

I am the King of the fields, and the King
  Of the town.

*Now We Are Six*

If I had a ship,
I'd sail my ship,
I'd sail my ship
Through Eastern seas.

*When We Were Very Young*


[5]

When he had finished hugging Christopher Robin,
and he nudged Piglet, and Piglet nudged him,
they thought to themselves what a lovely surprise
they had got ready.

*The House at Pooh Corner*


[6]

I'm as clever as clever.

*Now We Are Six*

"I'm planting a haycorn, Pooh, so that it can grow up into an oak-tree, and have lots of haycorns just outside the front door instead of having to walk miles and miles, do you see, Pooh?"

*The House at Pooh Corner*

Binker—what I call him—is a secret of my own,
And Binker is the reason why I never feel alone.

*Now We Are Six*

"Yes, those are dragons all right," said Pooh.
"As soon as I saw their beaks I knew.
That's what they are," said Pooh, said he.
"That's what they are," said Pooh.

*Now We Are Six*

"Well done, Pooh," said Rabbit kindly. "That
was a good idea of ours."

*The House at Pooh Corner*

[11]

And he sits and thinks of the things they know,
He and the Forest, alone together—

*Now We Are Six*

[12]

Look at all the presents I have had.

*Winnie-the-Pooh*

He was going so fast that he bounced up again almost as high as where he was before—and went on bouncing and saying, "Oo!" for quite a long time—and then at last he stopped and said, "Oo, lovely!"

*The House at Pooh Corner*

[14]

He is quite a different person now he hasn't got his spurs on.

*When We Were Very Young*

[15]

"Do Tiggers like honey?"
"They like everything," said Tigger cheerfully.

*The House at Pooh Corner*

Half way between Pooh's house and Piglet's house was a Thoughtful Spot where they met sometimes when they had decided to go and see each other.

*The House at Pooh Corner*

[17]

. . . very glad to be Out of All Danger again.

*Winnie-the-Pooh*

[18]

Mind you don't get blown away, little Piglet. You'd be missed.

*The House at Pooh Corner*

Let it rain!
Who cares?
I've a train
Upstairs.

*Now We Are Six*

[20]

And sometimes when our fights begin,
I think I'll let the Dragons win . . .
And then I think perhaps I won't,
Because they're Dragons, and I don't.

*Now We Are Six*

[21]

If I were King of Timbuctoo,
I'd think of lovely things to do.

*When We Were Very Young*

Pooh's mind had gone back to the day when he
had saved Piglet from the flood, and everybody
had admired him so much; and as that didn't often
happen he thought he would like it to happen
again.

*The House at Pooh Corner*

[23]

He learns. He becomes Educated. He instigorates
Knowledge.

*The House at Pooh Corner*

[24]

Then I hold her very tight, and
Tell her not to be so frightened—
And she doesn't be so frightened any more.

*When We Were Very Young*

They would sit down for a little and wonder what they would do now that they *had* seen each other.

*The House at Pooh Corner*

[26]

"This is Tigger."

"What is?" said Eeyore.

"This," explained Pooh and Piglet together, and Tigger smiled his happiest smile and said nothing.

*The House at Pooh Corner*

[27]

He might do something silly, and I do love him so.

*Winnie-the-Pooh*

"Tigger is all right, *really*," said Piglet lazily.
"Everybody is *really*," said Pooh.

*The House at Pooh Corner*

**[29]**

If you give him a smile
Only once in a while
*Then he never expects any money!*

*When We Were Very Young*

**[30]**

It just happened to be Me.

*Winnie-the-Pooh*

# DECEMBER

But all the little wood was still,
As if it waited . . .

*When We Were Very Young*

I hope it won't snow.

*Winnie-the-Pooh*

[2]

A little Consideration, a little Thought for Others, makes all the difference.

*Winnie-the-Pooh*

[3]

I'll give you a Please
    And a How-do-you-do,
I'll show you the Bear
    Who lives in the Zoo.

*Now We Are Six*

. . . a Very Grand Thing to talk about afterwards.

*The House at Pooh Corner*

[5]

Oh, I like his way of talking,
    Yes, I do.
It's the nicest way of talking
    Just for two.

*The House at Pooh Corner*

[6]

So he decided to do something helpful . . .

*Winnie-the-Pooh*

I've found somebody just like me. I thought I was the only one of them.

*The House at Pooh Corner*

[8]

It's his party, because of what he did, and I've got a present for him and here it is.

*Winnie-the-Pooh*

[9]

He's a clever sort of man.

*Now We Are Six*

I want some crackers,
    And I want some candy;
I think a box of chocolates
    Would come in handy;

*Now We Are Six*

[11]

Just for a moment, she thought she was frightened,
and then she knew she wasn't.

*Winnie-the-Pooh*

[12]

Poetry and Hums aren't things which you get,
they're things which get *you*.

*The House at Pooh Corner*

Hand in hand we come
 Christopher Robin and I.

*Winnie-the-Pooh*

[14]

Sometimes Winnie-the-Pooh likes a game of some sort when he comes downstairs, and sometimes he likes to sit quietly in front of the fire and listen to a story.

*Winnie-the-Pooh*

[15]

I feel that we all should do what we can to help.

*Winnie-the-Pooh*

It's dangerous, but I can do it all right.
*The House at Pooh Corner*

[17]

Brains first and then Hard Work.
*The House at Pooh Corner*

[18]

The more it snows
       (Tiddely pom),
The more it goes
       (Tiddely pom),
The more it goes
       (Tiddely pom),
    On snowing.
*The House at Pooh Corner*

And I sometimes call him Terrible Jack,
'Cos his tail goes on to the end of his back.

*When We Were Very Young*

[20]

Every one says, "Run along,
There's a little darling!"

*Now We Are Six*

[21]

If you try to talk to the bison, he never quite understands.

*When We Were Very Young*

He Knows Things.

*Winnie-the-Pooh*

[23]

"I'm not asking anybody," said Eeyore. "I'm just telling everybody."

*Winnie-the-Pooh*

[24]

And, oh! Father Christmas, if you love me at all,
Bring me a big, red india-rubber ball!

*Now We Are Six*

And people seized their stockings,
  And opened them with glee . . .

*Now We Are Six*

[26]

AND OH, FATHER CHRISTMAS,
MY BLESSINGS ON YOU FALL
    FOR BRINGING HIM
    A BIG, RED,
    INDIA-RUBBER
    BALL!

*Now We Are Six*

[27]

He climbed a little further . . . and a little further
. . . and then just a little further.

*Winnie-the-Pooh*

. . . never let things come to him, but always went
and fetched them.

*The House at Pooh Corner*


[29]

I often wish I were a King,
And then I could do anything.

*When We Were Very Young*

[30]

With a big brown furry-down up to my head,
I'd sleep all the winter in a big fur bed.

*Now We Are Six*

He uses short, easy words, like "What about lunch?"

*The House at Pooh Corner*

On this and the following pages you can keep many other Important Things to Remember. Perhaps you'll want to write the names of all your pets, or the titles of your favorite books.